West C

...ay
B&B Guide

1999/2000

Use this guide with the official route map
available from Sustrans 0117 929 0888

Gina Farncombe

Curlew Press

2nd Edition	*The West Country Way B&B Guide*
Published by	Curlew Press Croft House Newton Reigny Penrith Cumbria CA11 OAY Tel 01768 865435
e-mail no Web page	curlew@croftcot.u-net.com http://www.cumbria.com/ accom/cycling.htm **See Web site for new publications** © Curlew Press 1999
Printed by	Reeds Ltd.
Thanks to	Aidan Warlow
Drawings	Gina Farncombe
Distributed by	Cordee Books and Maps 3a De Montfort Street Leicester LE1 7HD Tel 0116 254 3579

CONTENTS

Accommodation place names

THE WEST COUNTRY WAY CYCLE ROUTE

BRISTOL & BATH

The route starts with the traffic-free stretch of the Camel Trail between Padstow and Bodmin and ends at the Bristol & Bath Railway path. Between the two lies the lovely Tarka Trail in North Devon. There are stretches of Canal tow paths and miles of quiet roads to be savoured by the cyclist along this quiet traffic-free route. Although climbs to Bodmin Moor, Exmoor and The Mendips are demanding, there are plenty of long downhill stretches throughout the cycle route.

Eclipse-seekers!

This is the first UK mainland solar eclispse for 70 years. A once in a life time experience! The best way to see it is of course from your bike. Let's hope August 11th 1999 is a cloudless day.

PADSTOW

HOW DO I START?

*You can go by train to Bodmin Parkway and then by bus for the 18 miles to Padstow or via the Steam Train to the Camel Trail. At the moment the bus only allows fold up bikes, but by the time you read this they may be taking all bikes, 'phone **01208 79898** for details. If it is essential that you come to Padstow by car it is possible to purchase a week-long parking ticket for £12.00 at either of the two car parks on the harbour front.*

GETTING THERE

TRAINS

Great Western provides services from London, Reading, South Wales & the Cotswolds

Bookings 0345 000 125

Bus Links 01209 719988

Wales & West Passenger Trains run direct passenger trains into Cornwall via Bristol from Manchester, Birmingham, Bath, Swindon & Cardiff

Bookings 0345 125 625

Virgin Trains operate services from Birmingham, Bristol, the North and Scotland

Bookings 0345 222 333

BUS & COACH

National Express serves Cornwall from over 1,200 cities and towns in the UK

Enquiries 0990 010104

Bookings 0990 808080

Western National

West Cornwall 01209 719988

North/mid Cornwall 01208 79898

Note for rail travellers arriving at Bodmin:

It is recommended that you travel by Bodmin & Wenford Steam Railway (Summer months) which takes you to the Camel Trail - bikes go free!

Steam Railway Enquiries: 01208 73666

TAXI-BUS SERVICE

Carries up to 3 bikes and passengers. Phone 01208 73000
For further details phone Bodmin TIC 01208 76616

THE WEST COUNTRY WAY CYCLE ROUTE - SOUTHERN HALF

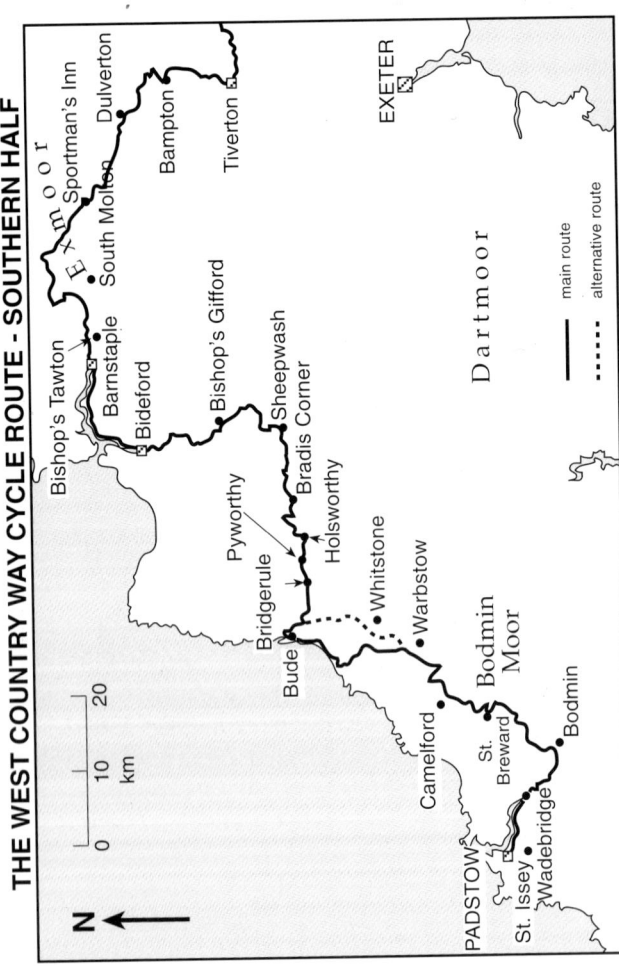

THE WEST COUNTRY WAY CYCLE ROUTE - NORTHERN HALF

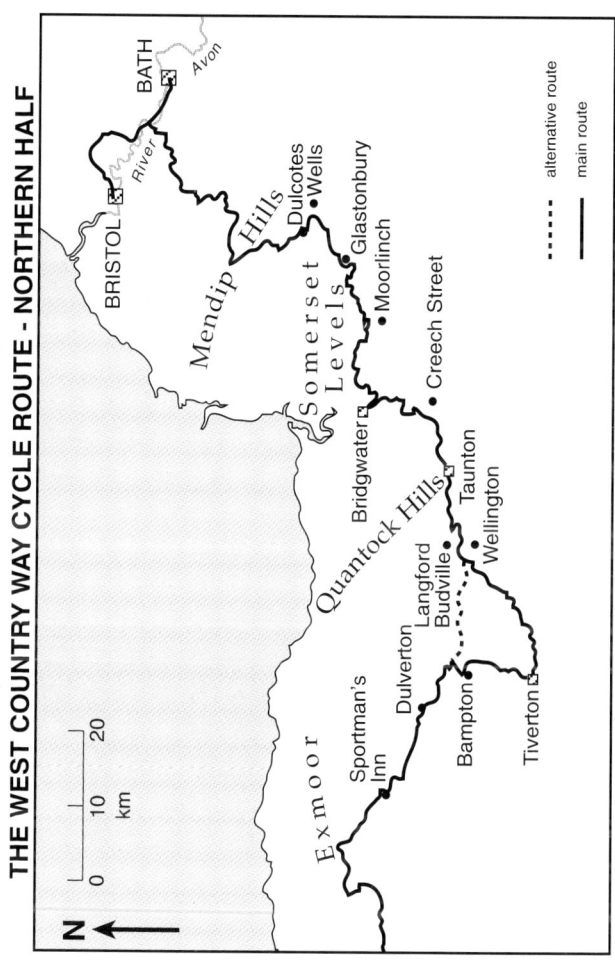

PADSTOW

Fishing thrives despite the gradual silting up of the Camel estuary. Small boats bring in crabs and lobster; the larger 'netters' catch cod and tuna in the Bay of Biscay. Trawlers bring in flat fish including turbot. Most of this is exported to France and Spain, but you can enjoy a full range of very fresh fish in the restaurants along the quayside.

Why did the estuary silt up? Legend has it that one day a mermaid was gently frolicking in the harbour when a trigger-happy local lad took a pot shot at her. In her fury, the mermaid put a terrible curse that the sand would always silt up the estuary at the point which is to this day known as Doom Bar !

If you happen to be around on May 1st and are wondering why people are behaving oddly, it will be the ancient pagan ceremony of the 'Obby 'Oss when folk dress in carnival gear and cavort through the streets making a loud noise! You are welcome to join in.

PADSTOW

PLACES OF INTEREST

Prideaux Place   Elizabethan home of the Prideaux-Brune family, overlooks Camel Estuary

EATING OUT

The Seafood Restaurant   Famous, delicious and expensive by the riverside 01841 532485

Brocks Restaurant   Wholesome food with value for money The strand 01841532565

CYCLE SHOPS

Brinhams   Cycle Hire and repairs 01841 532 594

Padstow Cycle Hire   South Quay 01841 533533

The Camel Trail

The name is derived from 'Cam' which means crooked and 'Heyle' meaning the mouth of an estuary or river - 'the crooked river!' The steam train from Waterloo first chuffed its way along the estuary in 1899 carrying visitors from the smoke of the capital to the clear air of the North Atlantic coast.

Almost 100 years later it is a safe traffic-free path from which to enjoy the spectacular view of the Camel Estuary and surrounding landscape.

9

Padstow

Linda and Les Green Roselyn, 20 Grenville Road, Padstow, Cornwall PL28 8EX

Telephone/Fax	**01841 532756**
Rooms	1 twin + 1 single + 1 double/family
B&B	£20.00-£25.00 *(all en-suite)*
Packed lunch	Available *(prior notice please)*

(No smoking please.) **AA QQQ Recommended.** *"10 mins walk from train and town centre. Garage for bicycles, on-site safe parking. Varied breakfast menu including vegetarian. All rooms colour TV, tea/coffee-making facilities, hairdryers."*

Gary Clark Treverbyn House, Station Road, Padstow, Cornwall PL28 8DA

Telephone	**01841 532855**
Rooms	3 double *(all en-suite)*
B&B	£28.00
Packed lunch	Available
Eating out	Walking distance

Highly Commended. *"Elegantly furnished Edwardian house with open fires. All rooms have beautiful estuary views, room service, colour TV, and tea/coffee-making facilities."*

St Issey

Alice and Bryan Mealing Trevorrick Farm, St Issey, nr Padstow, Cornwall PL27 7HQ

Telephone	**01841 540574** Fax 01841 540834
Rooms	3 double *(all en-suite)*
B&B	£18.00-£33.00
Evening meal	£11.00 *(prior notice please)*
Packed lunch	Available *(prior notice please)*

(No smoking in bedrooms please.) **2 Crowns Commended.** *"Comfortable old stone farmhouse about 1 mile from Camel Trail. TV, tea/coffee-making facilities. Evening meal by arrangement. Heated indoor swimming pool, games room."*

WADEBRIDGE

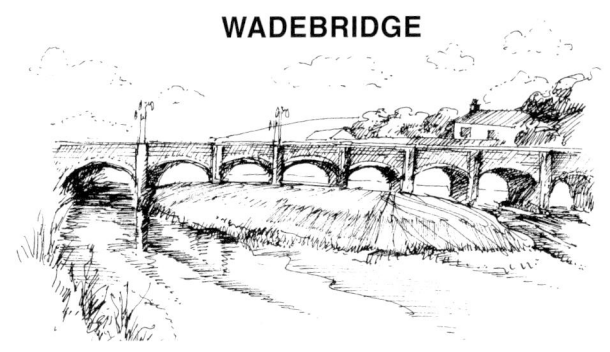

Wadebridge is an old sea port on the tidal reaches of the Camel. It was the home of the late Poet laureate, Sir John Betjeman. The river Camel played an important part in the town's early prosperity as all manner of cargoes would have travelled by boat. In earlier days the roads were very poor. The bridge, which must have revolutionised life in the town, was built by the Reverend Lovibond in 1460 and has seventeen arches across its 320ft length. Legend has it that it was built on wool sacks or bales, but it seems more likely that this refers to the finance for the bridge coming from wool merchants and sheep farmers.

PLACES OF INTEREST
Betjeman Centre   Old Station waiting room

PLACES TO EAT
The Earl of St. Vincent   Egloshayle 01208 814807

BIKE SHOPS & REPAIRS
Bridge Cycle Hire   Eddystone Road 01208 814545
Bridge Bike Hire   Eddystone Road 01208 813050

Wadebridge

Stephen and Jenny Knightley	Spring Gardens, Bradfords Quay, Wadebridge, Cornwall PL27 6DB
Telephone	**01208 813771**
Rooms	1 single + 2 double
B&B	£15.00-£20.00
Evening meal	No
Packed lunch	£3.50
Eating out	Walking distance

(No smoking please.) "Grade II Listed Georgian detached family home in the centre of Wadebridge, right on the river and the famous Camel Trail."

Angus Lamond	Arcadia, St. Breock, Wadebridge, Cornwall PL27 7JS
Telephone/Fax	**01208 814572**
Rooms	1 double + 1 family + *studio for family*
B&B	£10.00-£16.00
Evening meal	No Packed lunch £3.00
Eating out	Walking distance

(No smoking please.) "Cottage accommodation in idyllic and quiet wooded valley next to 1,000 year old church. 3/4 mile to Camel Trail. Good pub & supermarket nearby."

Bodmin

John and Ann Cornish	Westberry Hotel, Rhind Street, Bodmin, Cornwall PL31 1NZ
Telephone	**01208 72772**
Rooms	3 single + 20 double *(most en-suite)*
B&B	£20.00-£28.00
Evening Meal	£12.00 Packed lunch £3.50

"19th-c building situated in town centre. Colour TV, radio and telephone."

St Breward

Mr and Mrs L Turner 'Tarny Guest House', St Breward, Bodmin, Cornwall PL30 4LW

Telephone	**01208 850583**
Rooms	2 family + 2 double *(some en-suite)*
B&B	£16.00-£20.00
Packed lunch	£3.00 Eating out walking distance

(No smoking please.) **WCTB ETB 2 Crowns Commended.**
"Warm and friendly. TV and tea/coffee-making facilities in all rooms. Acres of private gardens, woods, waterfalls, magnificent views. In area of outstanding beauty, ideal for touring the coast and moor. The West Country Way runs through St Breward. Local shop and PO 200 yds."

John and Veronica Stansfield East Rose Farm, St Breward, Bodmin Moor, Cornwall PL30 4NL

Telephone	**01208 850674**
6 Holiday Cottages	Sleep 2-7, £18.00 per cottage per night
Packed lunch	Wide choice available
Eating out	1¼ miles

"A remote moorland farmstead on the West Country Way/ Route 3 between Blisland and St Breward above the Delphy Bridge. Lunches, cream teas and light refreshments always availbale. Small shop, payphone and laundry facilities. 5 lakes with superb coarse fishing, cycle hire and spares."

Bodmin Moor

Camelford

Mrs A Hopkins	Trenarth, Victoria Road, Camelford, Cornwall PL32 9XE
Telephone	**01840 213295**
Rooms	1 family + 1 double + 1 single room
B&B	£16.00
Pub	Half a mile to Camelford
Distance from route	Very near

"A warm welcome awaits you at Trenarth. Wonderful views toward Bodmin Moor from bedroom."

Mrs Gillian Stiles	Carcade Farm, Camelford Cornwall PL32 9XG
Telephone	**01840 212288**
Rooms	1 double + 1 twin + 1 single
B&B	£16.00
Evening meal	£8.00 *(prior notice please)*
Packed lunch	Available *(prior notice please)*

(No smoking in bedrooms please.) "Period farmhouse north side Bodmin Moor on spur of cycle path close to Roughtor and Davidstow. Names on OS maps.

Warbstow

Richard and Gill Grigg	Fentrigan Manor Farm, Warbstow, Launceston, Cornwall PL15 8UX
Telephone	**01566 781 264**
Rooms	2 double + 1 single
B&B	£15.00-£18.00
Evening meal	£8.00 Packed lunch £2.50
Pub	3 miles

"16th-c manor house on working farm, peaceful and beautiful surroundings. Warm welcome for weary cyclists, hearty breakfasts and home-cooking. ½ mile from cycle route."

BUDE

Bude has been a popular but very respectable holiday centre since Victorian times. Not long ago it was renowned for its shipwrecks. There were no less than eighty in this area between 1824 and 1874! They have now got a very solid high-tech lifeboat which is open for visits from the public. Widemouth Bay, an area of 'outstanding natural beauty', is famous for its magnificent golden beach and it attracts windsurfers, wave skiers and surfboarders from all over the UK to come and enjoy its sometimes vast Atlantic rollers. An added attraction is a major international Jazz Festival at the end of August.

PLACES OF INTEREST
Canal Life Boat House   Bude and Stratton Museum

PLACES TO EAT
Bistro Italiano   Town Centre 01288 355 973

BIKE SHOPS & REPAIRS
North Coast Cycles   Ocean View Rd 01288 352974

Bude

Jeannette Evans-Gittins	Clovelly House, 4 Burn View, Bude, Cornwall EX23 8BY
Telephone/Fax	**01288 352761**
Rooms	2 single *(standard)* + 4 double *(en-suite)*
B&B	£15.00-£23.00
Evening meal	£3.75-£7.50
Packed lunch	£2.50 *(no smoking in bedrooms please)*
Eating out	Walking distance

ETB 2 Crowns Commended. *"Enjoy a friendly home from home atmosphere in this well located town house opposite the Golf Club, in the town, and less than 1 minute from the sea. Ideally placed for exploring the dramatic Atlantic coast and beautiful beaches. TV and tea/coffee-making facilities."*

Dennis and Jane Rouse	Corisande Hotel, 24 Downs View, Bude, Cornwall EX23 8RG
Telephone/Fax	**01288 353474**
Web	http://www.scoot.co.uk/corisande-hotel
Rooms	6 double + 1 twin *(most en-suite)*
B&B	£15.50
Evening meal	£10.00 Packed lunch £3.50
Pub	200 yds
Distance from route	On route

ETB 3 Crowns. *"Licensed hotel, real 'home from home', full central heating. Excellent home-cooking, indoor storage for bikes, close to town centre."*

Marhamchurch

Mrs Mary
 Trewin

Court Farm, Marhamchurch,
Bude, Cornwall EX 23 0EN

Telephone   **01288 361494**
E-mail   court-farm@n.direct.co.uk
Rooms   4 double en-suites + 1 double
B&B   £17.00-£20.00 *(all en-suite)*
Packed lunch   £3.00 *(pre-book please)*
Eating out   Pub 15 yds
Distance from route   On route

(No smoking please.) **2 QQQ.** *"Lovely 16th-c farmhouse in centre of pretty Cornish village. All rooms with TV, tea/coffee-making facilities. Heated indoor swimming pool Easter-November. Drying facilities available."*

Widemouth Bay

Bridgerule

Mrs Margaret Jones	Holladon Farm, Bridgerule, Holsworthy, Devon EX22 6LN
Telephone	**01288 381268**
Rooms	2 double + 1 twin
B&B	£16.00-£18.00
Evening meal	£8.00 Packed lunch £3.00
Pub	1½ miles

(No smoking please.) *"Pleasantly situated working farm just off cycle route. Comfortable, with lovely views. Tea/coffee-making facilities, TV. Garage for bikes etc. Good food."*

David and Vivienne Hale	Lodgeworthy Farm, Bridgerule, nr Holsworthy, Devon EC22 7EH
Telephone	**01288 381351**
Rooms	2 single + 3 double *(some en-suite)*
B&B	£17.00-£20.00
Evening meal	£10.00
Packed lunch	£3.00
Pub	Nearby

(No smoking please.)

ETB 2 Crowns Commended. *"Delicious home-cooking for all diets. Laundry facilities. Guests welcome to explore 200 acre dairy farm, set in beautiful countryside, with fishing. Garage for bicycles. On cycle route."*

HOLSWORTHY

This ancient little town has an important livestock market that dates back 700 years. It took place in the main square until the 1940's when, rather sadly, it was moved to the edge of town.

There is still a town crier, though he's not kept very busy nowadays. A curious ancient festival takes place on St Peter's Day beginning with the Pretty Maid ceremony. Nobody is allowed to know who the chosen maid is until the rector brings her out of the church door at the stroke of mid-day.

PLACES OF INTEREST
Pannier Market   Every Wednesday

PLACES TO EAT
The White Hart   Town centre 01409 253 475
John Henrys   Town centre 01409 253099

BIKE SHOPS & REPAIRS
Gifford Cycle Hire   12 Victoria Sq 01409 254020

Brandis Corner

Bickford Arms

Keith and Laura Phipps	Bickford Arms, Brandis Corner, nr Holsworthy, Devon EX22 7XY
Telephone	**01409 221318** Fax 01409 221781
Rooms	5 single + 5 double *(all en-suite)*
B&B	£25.00-£30.00
Evening meal	£5.95-£16.00
Packed lunch	£3.50 Distance from route 500 yds

(No smoking in bedrooms please.) **3 Crowns Commended.**
"17th-c inn set in quiet surroundings. All rooms en-suite with TV, video, tea/coffee-making facilities and direct dial telephones. Full English breakfast."

Holsworthy

Kay Gillard	Dormy House, Bude Road, Holsworthy, Devon EX22 7HZ
Telephone	**01409 253634**
Rooms	1 single + 2 double/twin
B&B	from £15.00
Evening meal	No
Packed lunch	£3.00
Pub	2 miles

"Friendly, comfortable home. Tea/coffee-making facilities in rooms, separate guest lounge, secure place for bikes."

Holsworthy

Mrs Elizabeth Venner	Penrose Villa, Bodmin Street, Holsworthy, Devon EX22 6BB
Telephone	**01409 253693**
Rooms	1 single + 1 twin + 1 double/family
B&B	£16.00
Pub	25 yds

(No smoking please.) "Friendly family guest-house on cycle route, in town centre, with large garden and lock-up for bikes. Full English breakfast. All rooms with colour TV and tea/coffee-making facilities. A warm welcome assured."

Whitstone

Mrs P Hopper	West Nethercott Farm, Whitstone, nr Holsworthy, Devon EX22 6LD
Telephone	**01288 341394**
Rooms	2 family + 1 double
B&B	from £15.00
Evening meal	Available Packed lunch £3.00
Pub	500 yds
Distance from route	1 mile

"A homely welcome on a working diary farm awaits you. Good home cooking, full English breakfast.

Pyworthy

Mrs Gillian Aston	Little Knowle Farm, Pyworthy, Holsworthy, Devon EX22 6JY
Telephone	**01409 254642**
Rooms	1 single + 1 twin + holiday cottage
B&B	£16.00-£20.00
Evening meal	£5.00 *(prior notice please)*
Packed lunch	£3.00
Pub	Walking distance *(lift available)*

"Friendly, informal working dairy farm on cycle route. Complimentary tea on arrival. Special diets catered for. TV. Laundry/drying facilities. Secure store for bikes. Camping available, flush toilet, running water. Open all year."

Sheepwash

Charles and Benjie Inniss

	Half Moon Inn, Sheepwash, Beaworthy, Devon EX21 5NE
Telephone	**01409 231376** Fax **01409 231673**
Rooms	2 single + 14 double *(all en-suite)*
B&B	£27.50-£38.50
Evening meal	£19.50
Packed lunch	£4.75

ETB ****. *"Small country hotel and village inn famous for its hospitality, good food and well-kept ales. Wide range of bar snacks every lunch time. Bike storage available."*

Jill and Brian Thomas

	Mermaid House, The Square, Sheepwash, Beaworthy EX21 5NE
Telephone	**01409 231213**
Rooms	1 single + 2 double
B&B	£17.50
Packed lunch	£3.50
Pub	100 yds

(No smoking please.)

"Attractive Grade II Listed house incorporating village stores on village square. Very comfortable rooms. Warm welcome awaits you, however wet and muddy!"

BIDEFORD

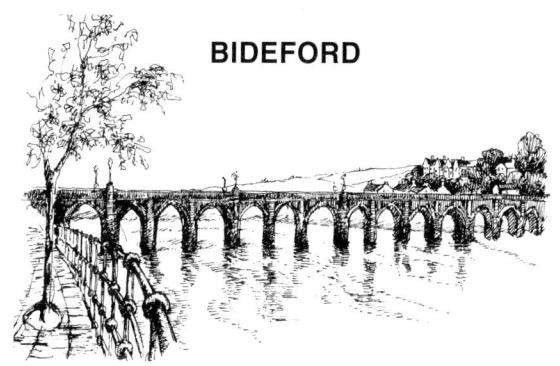

In Elizabethan times Bideford was a major seaport importing most of the country's tobacco from America. The narrow streets contain some fine old merchants' houses, particularly Bridgeland Street. The splendid bridge over the River Torridge is 677ft long and has strangely irregular arches. This is because the original bridge was built of oak and the arches varied according to the length of timber they used! The stone bridge has been faithfully copied.

PLACES OF INTEREST

Lundy Island   2 hour boat trip to a traffic-free environment - highly recommended

The Pannier Market   Sells local produce and crafts

EATING OUT

The Boathouse   Marine Parade 01271 861 292
Royal Hotel   Town Centre 01237 472 005

BIKE SHOPS & REPAIRS

Bideford Cycle Hire Torrington Street 01237 424123

Bideford

Mrs C. Stone

The Corner House, 14 The Strand, Bideford EX39 2ND

Telephone	**01237 473722**
Rooms	2 double + 1 single + 1 twin
B&B	£16.00
Evening meal	£8.00
Pub	Walking distance

"Our aim is to provide clean and comfortable accommodation in a friendly and warm atmosphere. Vegetarians and children are welcome."

Janet Taylor

Northdown Road, Bideford EX39 3LP

Telephone	**01237 473748**
Rooms	3 double + 2 single + 1 family + 2 twin
B&B	£20.00-£23.00
Evening meal	No *(own license)*
Packed lunch	£3.00
Pub	Walking distance

"A warm welcome, comfort and good food await you in this charming old Georgian hotel."

Weare Giffard

Mrs M. Ellison

Riversdale, Weare Giffard, Bideford EX39 4QR

Telephone	**01237 423676**
Rooms	2 double + 2 single
B&B	£20.00-£22.00
Evening meal	No
Pub	Walking distance

"200 year-old farmhouse within its own grounds. Only 1 mile from the cycling route. Laundry and drying facilities."

BARNSTAPLE

The Tarka
Trail

This is one of the most ancient towns in England minting its own coins in the 10th century. It was an important sea port until the river estuary silted up. In the 18th century it became rather smart and many of the prosperous merchants' houses survive from that period. The Long Bridge crossing the River Taw was thought to have been built in the 12th and 13th centuries. Barnstaple is famous for its magnificent displays of flowers. There is a pannier and craft market on Tuesdays and Fridays and a large cattle market every Friday.

PLACES OF INTEREST
The Butterfly House   Tropical butterflies in a miniature jungle. Ashford Garden Centre

Leisure Centre   Swim off those aches and pains! 01271 373361

EATING OUT
The Bank   Boutport Street 01271 324446
Chambers Brasserie   The Square 01271 321045

BIKE SHOPS & REPAIRS
Tarka Trail Cycle Hire   British Rail Station
01271 324202

Bishop's Tawton

Mrs J.R. Bater	Overton House, Codden Hill, Bishops Tawton, Barnstaple EX32 0DX
Telephone	**01271 342514** Fax **01271 375971**
Rooms	2 double *(with sauna or Jacuzzi)*
B&B	from £17.00-£25.00
Pub	nearby
Packed lunch	£3.00-£3.50

"Some parts of Overton House date back to the 15th-c. Lovely mature gardens and orchard. The house overlooks the Tor valley and is within 8 minutes bike ride from Barnstaple and the Tarka Trail. Mrs Bater is a massage therapist - say goodbye to those aches and pains!"

South Molton

John Adie	Barkham, Sandyway, South Molton, North Devon EX36 3LU
Telephone	**01643 831370**
E-mail	adie.exmoor@btinternet.com
Internet	www.btinternet.com/adie.exmoor
Rooms	1 double + 1 twin (1 room en-suite)
B&B	£20.0-£25.00
Evening meal	£16.00 Packed lunch £3.50
Pub	1 mile
Distance from route	150 yds

(No smoking please.) **AA QQQ.** *"Rambling Georgian family farmhouse in a lovely private Exmoor valley. Interesting dinners, comfortable beds, large drawing room and licenced."*

EXMOOR

In the Middle Ages the forest was one of many un-enclosed, uncultivated tracts of land where game, notably red deer, was preserved for the royal hunt. By 1300 the Royal Forest had been reduced from its original 200,000 acres to 20,000 and in 1818 the last 10,000 acres was sold to John Knight, a midlands ironmaster for only £5.00 an acre! Today local farmers graze cattle, sheep and of course the wild ponies on the moor.

The ponies *- Exmoor ponies, brown, bay or dun in colour, have a characteristic 'mealy-coloured' muzzle and inside ear. The quick intelligence and distinctive head show clearly the Exmoor pony's direct descent from the horses of pehistory.*

Sportsman Inn

The Proprietor	The Sportsmans Inn, Sandyway, South Molton, North Devon EX36 3LU
Telephone	**01643 831109** Fax **01643 831536**
Rooms	1 single + 2 double
B&B	£19.00 *(single)* £17.50 pp *(double)*
Evening meal	From £5.00 Packed lunch No
Pub	On site

"Traditional family-run rural inn set in the heart of Exmoor. Log fire, local real ales and good pub food. Secure cycle parking. Children welcome. Only 200 yds from route."

DULVERTON

After you leave the wilds of Exmoor the route suddenly descends to the unspoilt village of Dulverton nestling in a natural bowl in the landscape. It is surrounded by deciduous woodland and small Devonshire fields. There is a feeling of timelessness here. The main street and market square are surrounded by very attractive small Georgian houses and coloured-washed cottages.

PLACES OF INTEREST
Exmoor National Park
Information Centre   Town Centre 01398 323841

EATING OUT
Crispins   Imaginative home cooking
                            Town Centre 01398 323397

BIKE SHOPS & REPAIRS
Pedals   Town Centre 01398 324321

Dulverton

Mrs Carole Nurcombe

Marsh Bridge Cottage, Dulverton, Somerset TA22 9QG

Telephone	**01398 323197**
Rooms	3 double/twin *(2 en-suite)*
B&B	£16.00-£20.00
Evening meal	£11.50 Packed lunch £3.50
Pub	1 mile

"Superb accommodation on the banks of the River Barle. Delicious home-cooking, friendly informal atmosphere, luxury en-suite bathrooms, central heating, tea/coffee trays and lovely views. No smoking in bedrooms please."

Mr J. Everitt

Lion Hotel, Bank Square, Dulverton, Somerset TA22 9BU

Telephone	**01398 323980**
Rooms	4 single + 9 double/twin
B&B	£25.00-£28.00 (all en-suite)
Evening meal	£4.20-£10.00 Packed lunch £2.50

AA **. *"Ideally located for Exmoor, The Lion offers a cosy lounge with real ales and fine wines to enjoy with your food."*

Mrs Toni Jones

The Carnarvon Arms Hotel, Dulverton, Somerset TA22 9AE

Telephone	**01398 323302** Fax 01398 324022
Rooms	3 single + 20 double
B&B	£40.00-£55.00
Evening meal	Available
Pub	Hotel has Public Bar

AA *** *"A very traditional sportsmans hotel with excellent food. 5 miles of salmon and trout fishing."*

Dulverton

Gillian Aldridge

Scatterbrook Farm, Hinam Cross, Dulverton, Somerset TA22 9QQ

Telephone	**01398 323857**
Rooms	1 single + 2 double/twin
B&B	£12.50-£15.00
Evening meal	£9.00 Packed lunch £3.00
Pub	2° miles

ETB Approved 1 Crown. *"Central heating, en-suite rooms. Children and dogs welcome. Good food, and a warm welcome awaits. On Transcan route. Camping also available, £2 per tent, flush toilet, running water."*

Hollam

J. G. Hooper

Northcombe Camping Barn, Northcombe Farm, Hollam, Dulverton, Somerset TA22 9JH

Telephone	**01398 323118** or **01258 857107**
Camping Barns	Water Mill: 2 dormitories max 15, £3.50
	Lodge: 2 dormitories max 22, £3.50
Camping	£3.50 per tent
Meals	Self-catering Pubs 1 mile

"1 mile from Dulverton. 2 barns - 1 barn sleeps 15, 1 barn sleeps 22. Separate bathrooms, showers on 20p meter. Large kitchen/living area with cooker, microwave and woodburner/open fire. Electric on £1 meter. Footpaths and bridleways linking up to Exmoor and down the Barle River Valley."

Bampton

Edward and Pauline Tanner
The Courtyard, 19 Fore Street, Bampton, Tiverton, Devon EX16 9ND
Telephone **01398 331536**
Rooms 1 single + 2 twin + 2 double + 1 family
B&B £15.00-£17.00
Evening meal Available   Packed lunch £3.00
Pub Nearby *(has own Licensed Restaurant)*
"Colour TV and tea/coffee-making facilities in all rooms. Some are en-suite, those without a bathroom have a wash-hand basin with hot and cold water."

Chris and Kathy Ayres
Manor Mill House, Bampton Tiverton, Devon EX16 9LP
Telephone **01398 332211**   Fax 01398 332009
Rooms 1 double + 2 double/twin *(all en-suite)*
B&B £21.00
Evening meal No   Packed lunch No
Pub 100 yds.
(No smoking please.) **2 Crowns Highly Commended.**
"Peaceful and welcoming 17th-c beamed miller's house in historic floral Bampton. Riverside location, close to amenities. Rooms en-suite with tea/coffee-making facilities, TV. Drying facilities."

John and Ross North
Seahorse Inn, Bampton, Devon EX16 9LN
Telephone **01398 331480**
Rooms 2 double *(both en-suite)*
B&B £18.00-£20.00
Evening meal £6.00-£10.00 Packed lunch £3.00
"Large 18th-c coaching inn serving meals every day. Safe storage for cycles."

TIVERTON

The Grand
Western
Canal

Tiverton grew rich on wool between the 13th and 17th-c. By the 18th-c it had become the greatest manufacturing town in the country together with Exeter. There were 55 fulling mills and no less than 700 woolcombers! Lace-making was introduced later by John Heathcoat from the midlands which became a major industry. Today the lacemaking has diversified into net making. It still remains a town well-able to look after itself financially.

PLACES OF INTEREST
Horse drawn barge trip   please book 01884 253345
Tiverton Museum   Lace displays 01884 256295

EATING OUT
Upstairs Downstairs   Wholefood cafe/restaurant
    Angel Terrace 01884 254778
Anvils Restaurant   Evenings only 01884 254997

BIKE SHOPS & REPAIRS
Mainards   Gold Street 01884 253979

Tiverton

Janet and Tony Evans Angel Guest House, 13 St Peter Street, Tiverton, Devon EX16 6NU

Telephone	**01884 253392** Fax 01884 251154
E-mail	cerimar@global.net.com
Rooms	1 single + 1 twin + 2 family *(2 en-suite)*
B&B	£16.00-£18.00
Packed lunch	£2.50 Pub 200 m
Distance from route	400 m

(Smoking in bedrooms only please.) **2 Crowns.** *"Comfortable Georgian house in conservation area of town with all facilities nearby including bicycle repairs. TVs and tea/coffee-making facilities in rooms."*

Mrs Rita Reader Lodge Hill Guesthouse, Lodge Hill Farm, Tiverton, EX16 5PA

Telephone	**01884 252907** Fax **01884 242090**
Rooms	2 family + 2 double
B&B	£19.50-£22.00
Evening meal	£11.50 Packed lunch Yes
Pub	1 mile

2 Crowns. *"Just one mile south of the centre of Tiverton on the A396, in a quiet and peaceful setting in the middle of the Devon countryside."*

Mrs Shirley Tapp Little Gornhay Farm, Tiverton, Devon EX16 6SN

Telephone	**01884 252946**
Rooms	1 family + 1 twin + 1 double
B&B	£16.00 *(less for children)*
Packed lunch	£3.50 Pub Nearby

"Friendly, comfortable B&B accommodation on working dairy farm. Tea/coffee-making facilities, visitors' lounge with TV. Good breakfasts for weary cyclists. Open April-October."

Wellington

C Ayre   Greenham Hall, Greenham,
                        Wellington, Somerset TA21 0JJ
Telephone   **01823 672603**
E-mail   peterayre@compuserve.com
Rooms   1 family + 2 twin + 3 double
                        (singles welcome)
B&B   £19.00-£25.00
Pub   1 mile

"Relaxing atmosphere in unique Victorian turreted family house. Beautiful garden, rural location. Informal, peaceful, worth the effort to get here! Excellent food at local pub."

Langford Budville

Jessica Crawley   Wellisford Manor Farm, Wellisford,
                        Langford Budville, Wellington,
                        Somerset TA21 0SB
Telephone/Fax   **01823 672272**
Rooms   2 twin + 2 double *(singles welcome)*
B&B   £17.50 *(No smoking please)*
Pub   1½ miles

"Friendly, comfortable farmhouse in area of outstanding natural beauty where we provide transport to the highly recommended local pub. Bike lock-up and laundry. Guests' own lounge." **(See advertisement on page 53)**

TAUNTON

Historically, Taunton's greatest hour was in 1685 when it was the centre of the Duke of Monmouth's rebellion against James II. Monmouth's motley army, equipped with more pitchforks than guns, was brutally defeated to the north of the town at the Battle of Sedgemoor. Their ghosts (some say!) are occasionally to be seen hanging in balls of light over the battlefield or as phantom horsemen with cloaks flying in the wind! There is an excellent heritage trail through the town and a bustling market is held here every Saturday.

The Taunton to Bridgwater Canal

PLACES OF INTEREST
**Somerset County
   Museum**   Town Centre
Town Heritage Trail   Town Centre

EATING OUT
Sanctuary Wine Bar   Good food and atmosphere
                               01823 257788 .

The Castle   Top awards for food
                               Castle Green 01823 272671

BIKE SHOPS & REPAIRS
The Bicycle Chain   St James Street 01823 252499

Creech Street

Mrs Wendy Bowthorpe

	Court Barton, Bull Street, Creech St. Michael, Taunton, Somerset TA3 5PW
Telephone	**01823 443436**
Rooms	1 family/twin + 1 double
B&B	£15.00 *(reductions for children)*
Packed lunch	£2.50-£3.50
Pub	200 yds

(No smoking please.) "Spacious 16th-18th-c family home on edge of village and Somerset Levels. Children welcome. 200 yds from route."

Hope and Mick Humphreys

	Creechbarn, Vicarage Lane, Creech St Michael, Taunton, Somerset TA3 2PP
Telephone	**01823 443955** *(no smoking please)*
E-mail	mick@humphreys.netkonect.co.uk
Rooms	3 double + sitting room + library/studio
B&B	£18.00-£27.00 *(reductions for children)*
Evening meal	£12.00 *(please pre-book)*
Packed lunch	£5.00 *(please pre-book)*

AA Selected QQQ. *"Lovely converted Somerset long-barn only 200 yards from the Easterley Bridge on the canal tow/ cycle path between Taunton and Bridgwater.*

Moorlinch

Mrs Joyce Palmer

	Hill Cottage, Moor Road, Moorlinch, Somerset TA7 9BU		
Telephone	**01458 210511**		
Rooms	1 twin + 1 double		
B&B	£16.50	Packed lunch	£3.00
Pub	¼ mile		
Distance from route	On cycle route		

(No smoking please.) "Secure cycle storage. On route. Friendly, comfortable 200 year old cottage with modern amenities."

GLASTONBURY

Glastonbury for most people means the stupendous folk/rock festival that attracts 100,000 dreamy young people to the area every July. Hundreds of years before that visitors poured into the town to pray at the holy sites so Glastonbury is very used to welcoming the spiritual-searching visitor.

It is still a wonderful experience to wander in the grounds of the ruined abbey and see where Joseph's staff was planted in the ground to grow into the Holy Thorn Tree. The whole area has a very special atmosphere, a place of pilgrimage to this day. You should also walk up on to the Tor, the 500ft conical hill on the edge of town. It has magnificent views and its own legendary atmosphere. Some say that King Arthur is buried deep within it - but he is not dead! One day he will emerge again to claim back his kingdom.

The Tor

PLACES OF INTEREST
Glastonbury Abbey   Town Centre
Glastonbury Lake Village   The Tribunal - exhibition of
  Museum   iron-age lake village - excellent

EATING OUT
The George & Pilgrims   High Street 01458 832252
Hawthorns Hotel   Northload Street 01458 831255

BIKE SHOPS & REPAIRS
Pedlers   Magdalene Steet 01458 831117

Glastonbury

Mrs Naomi Frost
Hartlake Farm, Hartlake, Glastonbury, Somerset BA6 9AB

Telephone	**01458 835406** Fax **01749 670373**
Rooms	1 double + 1 twin *(all en-suite)*
B&B	£18.00-£22.00
Packed lunch	£3.00 *(please pre-book)*
Pub	Walking distance

(No smoking please.) **2 Crowns Commended.** *"Cosy and relaxing break in 17th-c farmhouse just outside Glastonbury. Bountiful breakfasts served to start you on your way."*

Penny and David Riddle
Hillclose, Street Road, Glastonbury, Somerset BA6 9EG

Telephone/Fax	**01458 831040**
Rooms	3 double/twin
B&B	£15.00-£20.00
Pub	¼ mile

"Warm, friendly atmosphere, clean rooms, comfortable beds, full English breakfast. Just 4 mins walk to town centre and Abbey. Tea/coffee-making facilities and TV in all rooms."

Sylvia and Derek Hankins
Blake House, 3 Bove Town, Glastonbury, Somerset BA6 8JE

Telephone	**01458 831680**
Rooms	1 double + 1 twin *(en-suite showers)*
B&B	£16.00-£16.50
Packed lunch	£3.50
Pub	Nearby

(No smoking please.) *"Enjoy a welcome 'cuppa' in our listed 17th-c stone house. Close to town centre, all attractions and amenities."*

WELLS

This is the smallest city in England. It has a very busy shopping centre, but step into the Cathedral close and all is peace and piety. The medieval cathedral is magnificent both inside and out. The West front was once covered with nearly 400 statues of saints, prophets and angels and many of them are still there. Inside, look for the humorous carvings on the pillar capitals.

You can visit, but not enter, the romantic 13th-c Bishop's

Palace. On the left of the gatehouse you will notice a small bell with a rope attached. In the 19th-c a bishop's daughter taught a swan to ring this bell for food. To this day the swans of the moat have continued this charming tradition.

PLACES TO VISIT
Wells Cathedral   Wonderful medieval sculptures
Vicar's Close   Oldest inhabited 14th-c street in
                          Europe. Don't miss number 22!

EATING OUT
The Good Earth   Excellent vegetarian restaurant
                          Priory Road 01749 675096

BIKE SHOPS & REPAIRS
The Bicycle Company   High Street 01749 675096
The Cycle Shop   St Cuthberts St 01749 670868

Wells

Mrs Esme Winter	17 Priory Road, Wells, Somerset BA5 1SU
Telephone	**01749 677300**
Rooms	3 single + 3 double/family
B&B	£16.00-£17.50
Evening meal	No
Packed lunch	£3.00
Pub	2 minutes

(No smoking please.) "Large Victorian semi, few minutes walk from shops, pubs. Home-made bread and preserves. Safe space for bikes, off-street parking. Friendly and informal."

Dulcote

Ros Bufton	Manor Farm, Dulcote, Wells, Somerset BA5 3PZ
Telephone	**01749 672125**
Rooms	1 single + 3 double *(en-suite/private)*
B&B	£18.50-£24.00
Evening meal	For groups *(prior notice please)*
Packed lunch	£3.50
Pub	1 mile

(No smoking please.) "On the West Country Way route. Lovely old farmhouse with animals, superb views, excellent hospitality and a great breakfast. Recommended by Country Living Magazine in 'Special Places to Stay in Britain'. Lock-up for bikes."

BATH

The story of Bath all started in the year 860 AD when a young prince called Bladud caught leprosy and was promptly thrown out of his home. He became a swineherd, but then his pigs caught leprosy too! One day his pigs wallowed in a muddy pool and were instantly cured. When Bladud copied them he too was cured. He lived happily ever after and the pool was made famous! The romans built a bath house here. Then in the 18th-c Bath became very fashionable with the 'Smart set' and that is when the grand terrace houses were built.

PLACES OF INTEREST
The Roman Baths (Spa)   Town Centre 0891 141178
River and canal trip   River side 0891 360396

EATING OUT
"Firehouse"   2 John Street 01225 482070
The Hole in the Wall   16 George Street
                              01225 425242

BIKE SHOPS & REPAIRS
Avon Valley Cycles   Rear of Bath Spa Railway
                              Station 01225 446267
John's Bikes   80/84 Walcot St 01225 334633

Bath

Jenny Bennett   Kinlet Villa, 99 Wellsway,
Bath BA2 4RX

Telephone/Fax   **01225 420268**
Rooms   1 Double + 1 family + 1 single
B&B   £18.00 -£38.00
Eating out   Nearby
Packed lunch   £3.00 *(please book)*

1 Crown Commended. *"The ambience is friendly and relaxing and Jenny Bennett will take great pleasure in advising you on local attractions. Enjoy dinner in one of the many good restaurants nearby."*

The Holburne Museum - Bath

Catherine Andrew   Meadowland, 36 Bloomfield Park, Bath
BA2 2BX

Telephone   **01225 311079**
Rooms   3 double rooms
B&B   £25.00-£30.00
Eating out   Nearby
Packed lunch   £3.00

"Set in its own quiet secluded grounds yet only a short distance from the city centre. Meadowland offers a superby appointed ensuite accommodation for the discerning traveller"

BRISTOL

Bristol is one of the great maritime cities, made rich by its trade with America and East Africa. By the late 18th-c, the harbour had become a problem. The huge rise and fall of the Avon caused ships to become dangerously marooned at low tide so a Floating Harbour was built and a two mile New Cut for the Avon was dug. Unfortunately, the cost of building was so high that dock dues forced shipping to other ports and Bristol, as a port, started to decline.

PLACES OF INTEREST
Bristol Docks   City centre 0117 927 3416
The Suspension Bridge Clifton

EATING OUT
Mud Dock   40 The Grove 0117 9349734
                Vegetarian available
Arnolfini   16 Narrow Quay. 0117 929 9191
                Cycle parking available at both

BIKE SHOPS & REPAIRS
Mud Dock   40 The Grove 0117 934 9734
Bike Tech   12/14 Park St 0117 929 7368

Bristol

Mrs van der Velden   Coldharbour Guest House
                          66 Coldharbour Road, Redland,
                          Bristol BS6 7LZ
Telephone   **0117 942 0117 Fax 0117 942 2677**
Rooms   1 double + 1 family + 1 twin + 3 single
B&B   £20.00-£24.00
Pub   Nearby

"Centrally situated in a pleasant part of Bristol. Very near good restaurants and shops. Enthusiastic and warm welcome to cyclists."

City Museum & Art Gallery

John and Nell Moran   The Lawns Guest House, 91 Hampton
                           Road, Redland, Bristol BS6 6JG
Telephone   **0117 973 8459**
Rooms   1 double + 2 twin
                           + 1 family
B&B   £20.00-£24.00
Pub   Nearby

"A friendly, cheerful guest-house offering simple accommodation and good value for money. Situated in a quiet area, close to a good bus service into the city centre."

The Llandoger Trow

Youth Hostels

Youth Hostels seem to be few and far between in the West Country. The Hostels listed below are all within 7 miles of the route.

Treyarnon-Bay Youth Hostel
Tregonnan, Treyarnon, Padstow, Cornwall PL28 8JR
Under 18s £5.70 Adults £8.50 *(3 miles south of Padstow)*
Tel/Fax 01841 520322

Tintagel Youth Hostel
Dunderhole Point, Tintagel, Cornwall PL34 0DW
Under 18s £5.70 Adults 8.50 *(5 miles west of route)*
Tel 01840 770334 Fax 01840 770773

Boscastle Harbour Youth Hostel
Palace Stables, Boscastle, Cornwall, PL35 0HD
Under 18s £5.70 Adults £8.50 *(7 miles west of route)*
Tel 01840 250287 Fax 01840 250615

Instow Youth Hostel
New Road, Instow, Bideford, Devon, EX39 4LW
Under 18s £5.70 Adults £8.50 *(on route)*
Tel 01271860394 Fax 01271 860055

Youth Hostels

Exford (Exmoor) Youth Hostel
Exe Mead, Exford, Minehead, Somerset TA24 7PU
Under 18s £5.50 Adults £8.50
Tel 01643 831288 Fax 01643 831650

Street Youth Hostel
The Chalet, Ivythorn Hill, Street, Somerset BA16 0TZ
Under 18 £5.15 Adult £7.70 *(on route)*
Tel 01458 442961 Fax 01458 442738

Cheddar Youth Hostel
Hillfield, Cheddar, Somerset BS27 3HN
Under 18s £4.75 Adults £6.95 *(7 miles west of route)*
Tel 01934 742494 Fax 01934 744724

Bath Youth Hostel
Bathwick Hill, Bath, Avon, BA26JZ
Under 18s £6.30 Adults £9.40
Tel 01225 465674 fax 01225 482947

Bristol International Centre Youth Hostel
Hayman House, 14 Narrow Quay, Bristol, BS1 4QA
Under 18s £7.65 Adults £11.20
Tel 0117 9221659 Fax 0117 927 3789

Caravan and Camping Sites

Padstow
Dennis Cove Campsite   01841 532 349

Wadebridge
Little Bodieve Holiday Park   01208 812 323

Bodmin
Bodmin Camping and Caravan Club
Old Callywith Road   01841 532 349

Camelford
Juliet's Well Holiday Park   01840 213 302

Bude
Widemouth Bay Camping   01288 361 210

Bridgerule
Hedley Wood Camping Park   01288 381 404

Holsworthy
Old Mill House   01409 281 379

Pyworthy
Little Knowle Farm   01409 254642

Great Torrington
Greenways Valley   01409 281 379

Caravan and Camping Sites

Barnstaple
Brightley Farm   01271 8550 330

Dulverton
Northcombe Camping Barn
2 dormitories max 15 people £3.50pp
Camping available £3.50 per tent
Contact Mr J.G. Hooper   Tel 01398 323118
                          Fax 01258 857107

Tiverton
Samford Peverell
Minnows Caravan Park (on route)
Constant hot water. Modern heated toilet block
Contact Zig Grohala   01884 821770

Glastonbury
The Isle of Avalon Touring Caravan Park
Godney Road, Glastonbury
Sharon & Michael Webb   Tel/Fax 01458 833618

Priddy
Mendip Heights   01749 870 241

Bath
Newton Mill Centre   01225 333 909

Bristol
Baltic Wharf Camp Site
Cumberland Road   0117 926 8030

Tourist Information Centres

Padstow North Quay	01841 533 449
Wadebridge Town Hall	01208 813725
Bodmin	01208 76616
Camelford	01840 212954
Bude Crescent Car Park	01288 354240
Holsworthy	01409 254185
Bideford	01237 477676
Barnstaple	01271 375000
Dulverton	01398 323841
Exmoor Nat. Park	01398 323 841
Tiverton	01884 255827
Tiverton Motorway Services	01884 821242
Taunton	01823 336344
Bridgwater	01278 427652
Glastonbury	01458 832954
Wells	01749 672552
Bath	01225 477101
Bristol	0117 926 0767

Weather News

Devon and Cornwall	0891 500404
Somerset	0891 500405

Bike Shops and Repairs

Padstow
Brinhams Cycle Hire and repairs   01841 532 594
Padstow Cycle Hire   01841 533 533
Wadebridge
Bridge Cycle Hire   01208 814545
Bridge Bike Hire   01208 813050
Bude
North Coast Cycles   01288 352974
Holsworthy
Gifford Cycle Hire   01409 254020
Bideford
Bideford Cycle Hire   01237 424123
Barnstable
Tarka Trail Cycle Hire   01271 324202
Dulverton
Pedals   01398 324321
Tiverton
Mainards   01884 253979
Taunton
The Bicycle Chain   01823 252499
Glastonbury
Pedalers   01458 831117
Wells
The Bicycle Company   01749 675096
The Cycle Shop   01749 670868
Bath
Avon Valley Cycles   01225 446267
John's Bikes   01225 334633
Bristol
Mud Dock   0117 934 9734
Bike Tech   0117 929 7368

(Addresses of shops are listed under place names in text)

Eating out

Padstow
The Seafood Restaurant   01841 532485
Brocks Restaurant   01841 532565
Wadebridge
The Earl of St. Vincent   01208 814807
Bude
Bistro Italiano   01288 355973
Holsworthy
The White Hart   01409 253475
Bideford
The Boathouse   01271 861292
Barnstaple
The Bank   01271 324446
Chambers Brasserie   01271 321045
Dulverton
Crispins   01398 323397
Tiverton
Upstairs Downstairs   01884 254778
Anvils Restaurant   01884 254997
Taunton
Sanctuary Wine Bar   01823 257788
The Castle   01823 272671
Glastonbury
The George & Pilgrims   01458 832252
Wells
The Good Earth   01749 675096
Bath
Firehouse   01225 482070
The hole in the Wall   01225 425242
Bristol
Mud Dock   0117 9349734
Arnolfini   01179299191

(Addresses are listed under place names in the text)

*"Take nothing but photographs
Leave nothing but tyre-tracks"*

yha

Check List

Tool Kit

Chain splitter
Pump
Allen keys
Adjustable spanner
Screwdriver
Tyre levers
Spoke key
Strong tape (for quick repairs)
Chain & gear lubricant

Bike Spares

Puncture repair kit
Front and rear lights
Batteries
Spare chain links
Brake blocks
Straddle wire
Bike lock
Inner tube

Personal Kit

Wash kit
Money / credit card
Head torch
First aid kit
Liners for bags
Emergency rations
Water bottle
Survival bag
One change of clothi
Map & B&B Guide

Clothing

Towel
Cycle shorts (padded)
Cycle shirt/fleece top
Thermal vest
Helmet
Gloves
Fleece
Windproof top
Waterproof jacket
Waterproof trousers
Boots/shoes/trainers
Track suit bottoms
Underwear
3 pairs socks

Holiday Lakeland
Cycling Holidays

We provide you with full support for your
Sea to Sea Adventure (see inside front cover) and offers simi-
lar support for your ride on two other great adventures

The Nine Lakes Tour: This fascinating adventure is designed to combine the freedom to discover and explore the Lake District with comfort and style, each day taking you through new and exciting places of unspoilt beauty. 5 nights quality accommodation, route map and guide, luggage transfers, car parking and breakdown support. £195.00 per person. Cycle hire available.

The Reivers Route: Riding east to west, this route covers very different ground from the C2C and takes you over the border into Scotland. Our five night scheduled holidays @ £225.00 per person include transport to the start at Tynemouth, daily luggage transfers, car parking, and breakdown support. Cycle hire available. Private arrangements for 3 and 4 nights holidays are also available for experienced cyclists. Phone for details.

Tel: 016973 71871

or write to:

Holiday Lakeland Cycling
Dale View, Ireby, Cumbria CA5 1EA

Did you know?

* Twenty million cars are registered in Britain, and road traffic is projected to at least double by 2025.

* Vehicle traffic is the main cause of urban air pollution.

* 1 in 7 children suffers from asthma, thought to be exacerbated by traffic fumes.

* Over 1,500 wildlife sites, including 500 ancient wood-lands and at least 161 SSSI's are still threatened by road-building.

Join Sustrans! And help create a national network of Greenways...

Sustrans - means Sustainable Transport - has been building routes for cyclists and walkers for 15 years

It is now promoting a true National Network of traffic-free routes throughout Britain.
Please join the Sustrans Charity - help create a better way of life for us all.

Sustrans   35 King Street   Bristol   BS1 4DZ
0117 926 8893

sustrans

PATHS FOR PEOPLE

FOLLOW THE COUNTRY CODE

* ★ Enjoy the countryside and respect its life
* ★ Guard against all risk of fire
* ★ Fasten all gates
* ★ Keep dogs under close control
* ★ Keep to rights of way across farmland
* ★ Use gates and stiles to cross fences
* ★ Leave livestock, crops and machinery alone
* ★ Take your litter home
* ★ Help to keep all water clean
* ★ Protect wildlife, plants and trees
* ★ Make no unecessary noise

Helpful Comments Please !

If you have the time, we would be very interested to hear from you about any aspect of the guide and accommodation - constructive criticism is welcome! We are always looking for ideas to include in next year's guide, and for that ultimate West Country Way holiday photo for our next front cover.

_____

_____

_____

_____

_____

_____

_____

Please post to Curlew Press, Croft House,
Newton Reigny, nr Penrith, Cumbria CA11 0AY

63